THE PATH OF PRAYER

FOUR SERMONS ON PRAYER

PRAXIS

"Prayer is the elevation of the mind and heart to God in praise, in thanksgiving, and in petition for the spiritual and material goods we need. The Saviour commanded us to enter into our inner room, and there to pray to God the Father in secret. According to Saint Demetrius of Rostov, the inner room means the heart. Consequently, the commandment of the Lord obliges us to pray noetically to God in our heart. This commandment extends to all Christians. The Apostle Paul commands the same, saying that we must pray all the time in our nous.

"Paul commands mental or spiritual prayer for all Christians without exception. He also orders all Christians to pray unceasingly. To pray unceasingly is only possible in the heart. Therefore it is impossible to contest the fact that noetic prayer is compulsory for all Christians, and if it is obligatory, then it is also possible - God does not command the impossible."

Saint Theophan the Recluse

THE PATH OF PRAYER

FOUR SERMONS ON PRAYER

By Saint Theophan the Recluse

Introducing a personal rule of prayer.

Translated by Esther Williams, with a brief introduction by Margaret, Viscountess Long, and with a selection of prayers by the early fathers. Edited and compiled by Robin Amis.

PRAXIS INSTITUTE PRESS
A division of Praxis Research Institute,
an international non-profit corporation registered 1992 in the State of Massachusetts. Reg.No.043-110-773
PUBLISHED BY PRAXIS INSTITUTE PRESS
Three Barns, Aish Lane, South Brent, Devon TQ10 9JF, England   Tel: 01364 73205   Fax 01364 73889 e-mail:PraxPress@cs.com
Website www.praxisresearch.org

Second edition. Printed in Great Britain by
Booksprint, Wellington, Somerset

We gratefully acknowledge the help of the Russian Orthodox Church
in London in locating this translation.

British Library Cataloguing in Publication data:
A catalogue record for this book
is available from the British Library.
Saint Theophan the Recluse
THE PATH OF PRAYER

Library of Congress Catalogue Card Number:
91-60842

ISBN 1-872292-14-3 paperback
ISBN 1-872292-13-5 hard cover

FOUR SERMONS ON PRAYER

CONTENTS

PREFACE

Prayer for so many of us in the West is one dimensional and incomplete.

I remember sitting by the bed of my youngest daughter before she went to sleep. 'God bless Mummy and Daddy, Sarah and Jamie, Sugar Puff, Bramble, Jolly, Moth, Tumbleweed and Ophelia.' The prayers always ended with a list of ponies, dogs, cats and a tortoise. The only other time we prayed was for a few moments in church before the service began. It was a self-conscious bending forward with your head among the hymn-books, more of a social obligation than a prayer.

There was nothing particularly wrong with the prayers as far as they went, but they did not go far enough.

That prayer could be holy and profound, and the soul filled with grace and love and an almost tangible feeling of the Holy Spirit was something I never discovered until I found Orthodoxy. Then everything changed. There was a quality in prayer that it was difficult to describe in words. Like liquid flowing, you could not grasp it or show it to anyone. Veneration and contemplation meant so much more than simply asking for things.

In this tradition of Orthodoxy to which Theophan belonged we are helped to comprehend the abstract by the presence of icons. The perspective in the icon is back to front, widening into eternity rather than narrowing into worldly distance. Our vision expands, an understanding moves from the finite into an eternal dimension, the natural environment through which God can act. This forms the basis of a disciplined and progressive development of prayer as a true spiritual path.

This elusive quality, which is always so difficult to describe in words, is now given to us in these beautiful sermons by Saint Theophan. With instruction that is both simple and profound he prepares us for and leads us into true prayer and, if we are sincere enough, into the very presence of God.

Margaret, Viscountess Long of Wraxall

INTRODUCTION

FROM SPOKEN PRAYER
TO A HEART OF FIRE

For those who care about prayer but have never managed to get beyond the preliminaries, here are some answers from one of the Eastern Church's great masters of prayer, Bishop Theophan the Recluse - the saint canonized only in 1988, who lived and prayed less than a century ago, yet who speaks with the voice and the authority of the great fathers of the first centuries of the Christian Church.

At the same time as openly pointing out some of the difficulties in bringing prayer to life, this is a book that can genuinely provide assistance for those who want to make a serious beginning in prayer and are willing to make genuine effort for genuine results. Taken as a book of guidance, a book to study, these sermons about prayer are almost unique in providing a simple, accurate and in practical terms complete system of vocal prayer leading - although not without effort - from ordinary repetitive prayer to a truly contemplative life.

Metropolitan Antony of Sourozh, (Antony Bloom) once said, in one of his talks, that the Psalms provide a splendid source of words for those who need to express their feelings in prayer.

To Theophan, prayer has its own laws, and a rule - a way that works with these laws instead of against them - is needed if we are to achieve success in prayer. Theophan therefore suggests that this process begins from a recommendation similar to that made by Metropolitan Antony, writing that the great prayers of the Eastern Church, a millennium-long record of the prayers of great

1

and holy men, provide us with a rich seedbed of prayerful thoughts and images. Because they arise from hearts aflame with love of God, if these words are often repeated, he tells us, they can set our own hearts aflame, and do so far better than any theory about prayer.

This personal rule of prayer, as Theophan describes it, forms one of the great ways of spiritual development once listed as: the way of service, the way of prayer, the way of study and the way of self-control. It begins simply, from ordinary everyday prayer in church and at home - yet for those who are able to use this way it gains great power by borrowing from the prayers of far from ordinary men and women, forming the foundation of a simple but powerful way of prayer that - says Theophan, this *'mighty man of prayer,'* (as a monk of his time once described him) - will lead in time and with persistent practice to a complete and all-embracing life of prayer that, in the way of the fathers, is made spontaneous by a heart burning with love for Christ.

> *"Prayer is the elevation of the mind and heart to God in praise, in thanksgiving, and in petition for the spiritual and material goods we need. The Saviour commanded us to enter into our inner room and there to pray to God the Father in secret. According to Saint Demetrius of Rostov, the inner room means the heart. Consequently, the commandment of the Lord obliges us to pray mentally in our heart to God. This commandment extends to all Christians. The Apostle Paul commands the same, saying that we must always pray in our spirit.*

> *"Paul commands mental or spiritual prayer for all Christians without exception. He also orders all Christians to pray unceasingly. To pray unceasingly is possible only in the heart. Therefore it is impossible to contest the fact that mental prayer is compulsory for all Christians, and if it is obligatory it is also possible - God does not command the impossible."*

For those who understand what this implies, we need say no more. For those who do not, we cannot say more.

But because the prayers of the fathers are difficult to find in English translation, we have included at the back of this book some of the best of those classical Eastern prayers, as a source of help for those who are not familiar with these texts.

THE FIRST SERMON

A personal rule of prayer

When we pray, all our care should be focused on filling our souls with such emotion that when the tongue speaks in prayer, and the ear hears that prayer, and the body prostrates itself, the heart will not be found empty - but will be moved towards God by its emotion.

When such feelings are present, our prayer is prayer. When they are absent, it is not yet prayer.

It would seem that nothing could be more simple and natural for us than prayer in which the heart is turned towards God. Yet this is not always present in prayer, nor in everyone. It must be awakened, then strengthened; one must be educated even to achieve a spirit of prayer. The first step in this direction is to say prayers and to listen to prayers. If you say your prayers as you should, then you

5

will inevitably awaken in yourself a rising up of the heart toward God - and this is the way to enter into the spirit of prayer.

Our prayerbooks (Theophan, of course, refers to the prayer books used by the Orthodox Church in his time, and still in use today), contain the prayers of the holy fathers: Saint Ephraim the Syrian, Saint Macarius of Egypt, Saint Basil the Great, Saint John 'Golden Mouth' Chrysostom, and the other great masters of prayer. As they were themselves filled with the spirit of prayer, they put words to what the spirit revealed to them, and then they passed it on to us. Thus a great power of prayer moves in their every prayer. By the law of reciprocal action, those who enter energetically and attentively into these prayers will taste the power of the original prayer to such an extent that their spirit will come close to the spirit they contain.

* * *

To transform the way we say our prayers into a real education in prayer, they must be said in such a way that both heart and mind absorb their content. In order that you may achieve this, I will give you three simple instructions:

First, do not start to pray without at least some brief preparation;

Second, do not perform your prayer carelessly, but do so with attention and feeling;

Third, do not return to your usual occupations immediately you have finished praying.

Although prayer is a habitual action for us, it needs preparation. For anyone who knows how to read and write, what is more usual than reading and writing? Yet if we sit down to read or write, we do not do so suddenly. First we get ourselves into the mood for what we are going to do. This kind of preparation is all the more necessary before we start to pray, particularly if immediately beforehand we were occupied with something very different from prayer.

So, morning or evening, immediately before you begin to repeat your prayers, first stand for a while, sit for a while, or walk a little. Try to steady your mind, then turn it away from all worldly activities and objects. After this, think of who He is, Him to whom you turn in prayer. Next, recollect who you are; who it is who is about to start this invocation to Him in prayer. Do this in such a way as to wake in your heart a feeling of humility and reverent awe because you are standing in the presence of God.

All preparation for prayer consists in this reverent standing in the presence of God. To achieve this is a small task, but it is not one to be ignored. It is the beginning of [true] prayer, and a good beginning is half the complete task.

Once you have established your inner state in this way, stand before the icon and, prostrate yourself a few times. (Editor's note: If you are Protestant or Catholic, stand before the cross and kneel instead of prostrating.) Then begin the recital of the customary prayers. (For instance, you could repeat this prayer of the Eastern church: *'Glory be to Thee, Our God, glory be to Thee! O Heavenly King, Comforter, Spirit of Truth, come and abide in us....'*)

Repeat this without haste, so that you enter into every word, and so bring the meaning of each word down into your heart ... and accompany this by bowing. This is the whole work of prayer. It is fruitful and it is pleasing to God.

Simply enter into every word, then bring the meaning of each word down into your heart. That is, understand what you say, and then become aware of what you have understood. No further rules are necessary. These two, understanding and feeling - if they are properly carried out - ornament every offering of prayer with the highest quality, and this makes it fruitful and effective. For example, when you recite: *"and cleanse us from all impurities,"* experience with feeling your own impurity, desire to become pure, and pray to God in hope for it.

When you recite: *"and forgive us our trespasses,"* etc., first forgive everyone inwardly, and then, from a heart that has forgiven everyone for every single thing, beg the Lord to give us forgiveness.

When you recite: *"Thy will be done,"* submit your destiny to the Lord, and without questioning, state that you are prepared to accept willingly everything the Lord will send you.

If you work in this way at every line of your prayers, you will have said them in the correct manner.

* * *

To perform this work even more successfully, act in the following way:

1. Have your own rule of prayer, asking the blessing of your spiritual father for this. It should not be a lengthy rule, but one that you can perform without haste in the circumstances of your everyday life.

2. Before you pray, at a time when you have nothing else to do, read the prayers you will use. Make sure you understand and feel every word ... so that you know beforehand what should be in your heart at each and every word. It is even better to

8

learn all the prayers by heart. If you work in this way when you are saying your prayers, it will be easier for you to understand and to feel them. One difficulty will still remain: your mind will keep wandering off to attend to other things. What should be done in such a case?

3. It is necessary to make the effort to concentrate the attention, even though you know in advance that the thoughts will wander. When the mind does in fact wander during prayer, recall it again - and do so over and over again. Whenever you have said a prayer while your mind was wandering - and so have said it without feeling or comprehension - never forget to recite again everything that you said in this way.

If the mind wanders many times at the same place, repeat that section again and again. Do this until it is said entirely with feeling and understanding. Once you have overcome this difficulty, it may never repeat itself. If it does, it may not do so to the same extent - so this is the action to take when thoughts wander and you are distracted.

But it can also happen that some word will so strongly affect the soul that you will not wish to continue speaking the prayers. The tongue may continue to recite, but the mind will run back to the passage which affected it so powerfully.

* * *

In this situation:

4. Stop. Do not continue repeating prayers, but stand with your attention on those words [which moved you], feeling them. Feed the soul on them, or on the thoughts that arise from them. Do not hurry to move on from this state, even if you have no time left; it is better to leave your rule of prayer unfinished than to destroy this state of mind. This will sanctify you, and then perhaps it will last all day long, like the presence of the Guardian Angel. When you are saying prayers, this kind of action of grace means that the spirit of prayer itself is

9

beginning to penetrate into you ... and it follows that keeping such a state is the most hopeful way to encourage and strengthen the spirit of prayer within us.

Finally, once you have finished saying your prayers, do not immediately go on to do something else. Stand for a while, and consider what it is to which all this commits you. Try to hold in your heart what has been given you to feel during prayer.

Nobody who has fulfilled his rule of prayer with care will immediately want to return to his ordinary interests. This is the quality of true prayer! As our forefathers said, on their return from Constantinople: *"He who tastes sweetness does not then wish to taste something bitter."* This happens to everyone who has prayed conscientiously during his time for saying prayers. Indeed, you must realize that to taste this sweetness of prayer is the true aim of saying prayers, so if praying educates us and gives us a prayerful spirit, this happens precisely because of this tasting.

* * *

If you will be obedient to these few rules, you will soon see the fruits of this effort. Whoever fulfils these rules, even if they have not been given this instruction, will also taste this fruit.

Every repetition of prayer done in this way will leave a mark of prayer on the soul.

Uninterrupted practice in the order described will make it take root in the soul, and patience in this practice will establish a prayerful spirit.

May the Lord grant you this by the prayers of His most pure mother!

* * *

Here I have given to you the first elementary method of training the spirit in prayer in accordance with the aims of spoken prayer said at home in the morning and the evening - and in church.

But this is not all. Tomorrow I will tell you of another method.

AMEN

THE SECOND SERMON

Mental prayer

Yesterday, I showed you one method. By using it, you can educate the spirit of prayer in yourselves even while you are reciting the normal prayers from the prayer-book according to your personal rule.

But this is only the beginning of the art of prayer. You will need to go further. For example, you may recall the way you learn a language. First, the words and the forms of speech are learned by heart from books. But you cannot stop there. Instead, from this basis, you begin to move on to the stage where you can converse freely in the language you are studying.

You should do the same with the language of prayer. We become accustomed to reading our prayers from books - using the prayers passed down to us by Our Lord, and by the Holy Fathers who had achieved the art of prayer. But we must not stop at this. It is necessary to extend ourselves further. Once we have become

13

accustomed to turn our ears and hearts to God using this help given by others, we should then also attempt to bring something of our own to Him, so to speak; to pass on into our own prayerful conversation with God; to raise ourselves toward Him; to open ourselves to Him; to confess to Him the contents and needs of our souls.

But the soul must be taught to do this. I will point out to you briefly what must be done to succeed in this art ... but the habitual use of prayer books with reverence, attention and devotion leads to the same thing. Just in the same way that water pours of its own accord from an overfull vessel, so prayer to God begins to spring spontaneously from a heart which is filled with the holy feelings that have been produced by the habit of regular vocal prayer.

There are also special rules, special methods intended solely to achieve this objective, and everyone who wishes to succeed in prayer should become obedient to these rules.

Why is it, then, you may ask, that some people use their prayer books for years yet never have prayer in their hearts? To me, the reason for this seems to lie in the fact that the only time they make the effort to raise their hearts to God is while they are actually carrying out their rule of prayer ... only in the morning, for example. They think that then their relationship to God is complete, their duty fulfilled. After this, they spend their whole day in other activities, without ever turning to God. Then, when evening comes, they may decide it is time to turn back to the business of prayer.

So it happens that, even if the Lord does give them a good disposition in the morning, it will be smothered under the fuss created by the numerous activities of the day. This is the reason why they have no desire to pray in the evening. They have lost control of themselves, and are unable to soften their souls even to a small degree, so that prayer does not come easily, nor ripen easily. This is an all too common fault that needs to be put right, because one must act in such a way that the soul does not turn to God only when you are standing in prayer, but should do so as far as possible throughout the day. It should be an unceasing offering of oneself to Him.

To achieve this, it is necessary to begin - as often as possible during the day - by calling out to God from the heart in short words, according to one's needs and in ways appropriate to the events around you.

For example, whenever you begin something, say: *"O Lord, bless us."* On completing a task, say: *"Glory be to Thee, O Lord."* And do not only say these things with the tongue, but from the heart, with real feeling.

When passions rise in you, say: *"Save me, Lord, or I perish."* When the darkness of confusing thoughts begins to overcome you, call out: "Lead my soul out of imprisonment."

If you are attracted to an action that seems wrong, pray that He: *"Direct me back to the path, O Lord,"* or, *"do not let my steps be confused."*

If sins oppress you and plunge you into despair, call out with the voice of the publican: *"Lord, have mercy on me, a sinner ..."* Act in this way in every situation. Or you can simply say, as often as possible: *"Lord have mercy." "Holy mother of God, have mercy on me." "God's angel, my holy guardian, protect me."* Or make your appeal in other similar words. But do this as often as possible, always trying in every way to be sure that each ap-

15

peal comes from the heart, just as if it was actually squeezed from it. If you do this, you will frequently manage to consciously raise your heart to God, you will frequently turn to Him, you will pray frequently ... and this persistent repetition will end by forming in you the habit of conscious conversation with God.

But before we can make the soul appeal to God in this way, it first must be made to turn everything to the glory of God: to attribute to Him our every activity, large or small. This is the second method: this is how to teach the soul to turn to God as often as possible during the day. If we give ourselves the task of fulfilling the apostolic commandment, to do everything to the glory of God (I.Corinthians 10:31) - even eating and drinking - then we will inevitably remember God whatever we do ... and this not simply, but with circumspection, taking care that we do not act wrongly and do not trespass against God in any deed.

In turn, this will make us turn to God in fear, and to beg for his help and enlightenment. Then, because we are almost constantly doing something or other, we will find ourselves almost constantly turning to God in prayer - and in this we will be constantly practicing the art of uplifting the soul prayerfully towards God. But so that the soul may do this as it should - doing all things to the glory of God - it must be directed towards this from early morning onwards; from the very beginning of the day, before you go about your everyday business. Then it may last until evening.

This mood is induced by meditation on divine things ... and this is the third method of training the soul to turn more frequently towards God. Meditation is a reverent reflection on godly attributes and actions, and on what our glimpses of them demand of us. There can be reflection on the Goodness of God; on His Justice,

Wisdom, Might, Omnipotence - on His Providence, on His Dispensation to save us through the Incarnation, on His Mercy, on His Word, on the holy sacraments, on the kingdom of heaven.

* * *

Whichever of these aspects forms the basis of your reflections, it will inevitably fill the soul with reverent feelings towards God. You will discover that you are surrounded by God's mercies, bodily and spiritual. Then, if you are not a stone, you will find it necessary to fall before God - dissolved in humble feelings of gratitude.

If you begin to reflect on the Omnipotence of God, you will realize that nothing in yourself is hidden from his eye. Then you will resolve to be strictly attentive to the movements of your heart and your mind, in order that you should not trespass against the all-seeing God.

If you begin to reflect on the Truth of God, you will be persuaded that not one evil deed will remain unpunished, and so without doubt you will resolve to purify yourself of all your sins by means of heartfelt contrition and penitence before God.

Whatever quality or action of God you think of, if you meditate on it, your soul will fill with reverent feelings and a reverent attitude toward Him. This orients the whole being of a person directly towards God, and so it forms the simplest way to teach the soul how it should rise to Him.

* * *

The best, most appropriate time for this meditation is the morning, just after morning prayers, when the soul is not yet burdened by a multitude of impressions and cares.

When you have finished your prayers, sit down while your mind is still enlightened by prayer, and begin to reflect about some attribute or action of God: the first day about one, the next day about another. Think about it so that it gives rise to similar attitudes in your own soul. Saint Demitrius of Rostov said once: *"Come, holy meditation, and lead us to immerse ourselves in reflecting on the great deeds of God."* He would then dwell in his thoughts on God's plan and His creative actions, or on the miracles and suffering of the Lord our Saviour. In this way, he would move his heart, and so start his soul in an outpouring of prayer.

All of this can be done by everyone. There is no great labour needed, only desire and determination are necessary, and then the fruits will multiply of themselves.

So here are three methods you can add to the rule of prayer: methods by which you can teach the soul to rise prayerfully towards God.

To sum up, they are:
1. setting aside some time each morning to meditation on God;
2. turning every action to the glory of God; and
3. calling out often to God in brief appeals.

If your morning meditation on the divine is conscientious, you will find yourself with a lasting disposition to remember God.

By reflecting on God, you will make your soul careful to take account of God, and to act to His glory in its every action, outer as well as inner. And such a soul will be poised so that frequent prayerful exclamations will be drawn out of it.

These three: reflection on God; doing everything to the glory of God; and frequent appeals to God, are the most effective tools for prayer of mind and heart together. Each moves the soul towards God. The labour this involves can be compared to climbing a mountain. The higher up the mountain one is, the lighter and easier does one breathe. It is the same here: the more one accustoms oneself to these exercises, the higher he will raise his soul. The higher the soul rises, the more freely prayer will act within it.

Our soul is made to live in the mountainous world of God. That is where it should always dwell, both in thought and in heart. But the weight of worldly thoughts and passions attracts it and draws it downwards. The methods given here will detach it step by step from the earth, and in the end will detach it permanently. When this happens, the soul will enter its own proper sphere and will dwell blissfully in the heights. In feeling as well as in thought, and later in its very essence, it will be deemed worthy to stand before the face of God and dwell with the angels and the saints.

May the Lord in His goodness grant this to you all.

AMEN

THE THIRD SERMON

Unceasing prayer

I have already explained to you briefly two aspects, two stages of prayer. These are *spoken prayer*, when we pray to God with the prayers of others, and *mental prayer*, when we raise our mind to God through reflection on divine things. In this we offer everything to God, at the same time making frequent appeals to Him from the heart.

But even this is not all. There is a third stage of prayer, and this is genuine prayer. The first two are merely preparations for this. This can be described as: the constant turning of mind and heart to God. This is accompanied by inner warmth, and then by a burning of the spirit. This is the end which prayer should reach, and the aim which every worker in the spirit should keep in mind. Without it, we will labour in vain in the task of prayer.

Remember what is said about prayer in the Holy Word of God: *"Watch and pray."* (Matthew 26:41) says the Lord. *"Be sober, be watchful,"* teaches the apostle Peter (I Peter 5), *"continue stead-fastly in prayer, watching therein,"* (Colossians.4:2) and: *"with all prayer and supplication praying at all seasons in the Spirit,"* (Ephesians 6:18) the Apostle Paul instructs us. He explains elsewhere the reason why we should do this. It is because - he says: *"...your life is hid with Christ in God."* (Corinthians 3:3), *and "The Spirit of God dwelleth in you,"* (Corinthians 3:16) - *"to Him it is we call Abba, Father."*

From these exhortations and instructions you cannot fail to see that prayer is not some kind of casual, occasional activity, but should abide in us as an uninterrupted state of the spirit, just as breathing and the beating of the heart are uninterrupted actions of the body.

I will illustrate this with an example. The sun stands in the centre, and around it are all the planets; they are all attracted to it and turned towards it, some on one side, some on the other.

What the sun is in the world of objects, God is in the world of mind: the Sun of spirit. Turn your thoughts to heaven, and there, what will you find? The angels! According to the Lord's word, they always see the face of their heavenly Father. All the disembodied spirits, as well as all the saints in heaven, are turned towards God. All of them fix their mental eyes upon Him, and because of the inexpressible bliss which flows through them from this contemplation of God, they never wish to tear away their gaze.

We must learn to do on earth all this that is done by the angels and saints in heaven We must learn here to become accustomed to this angelic, continual, prayerful standing before God in our hearts.

Only someone who achieves this will become a true man of prayer. But how can one become worthy of this great gift?

I will answer this question briefly as follows: If you labour untiringly in prayer, always zealous and full of hope - if you strive without ceasing to reach the promised land, which is the burning of the spirit - you will certainly attain what you seek.

Saint Macarius of Egypt - who practised this work and received the fruits of prayer - testified to this fact.

"If you do not have prayer," he said, *"Labour in prayer. Then the Lord, seeing your work, will grant you this prayer, because of your patient perseverance, and because of your powerful desire for this blessing."*

Labour alone reaches only so far. But [it changes] when the fire is lit, that of which our Lord speaks as follows:

"I come to cast fire upon the earth," (Luke 12:49) *"and what will I do if it is already kindled."*

At this time, the labour comes to an end, and then our prayer becomes an easy, free and comforting flow.

But do not think that this describes some kind of very high state, one which cannot be approached by people in ordinary life. No. It actually is a high state, but it can be achieved by everyone. Everyone sometimes feels a warmth and ardour during prayer. This happens when the soul becomes detached from everything, enters into itself, and so prays to God with real warmth. It is actually during this occasional inspired descent of the Spirit upon prayer that the landmark of prayer may be reached, so that after this it becomes a constant condition.

23

As I have said, the way to this is to make efforts in prayer. When wood is rubbed against wood, it becomes hot, and in this way it makes fire. In the same way, when the soul is rubbed in the effort to pray, this friction finally evokes the fire of prayer.

The effort required for prayer consists of conscientiously persisting in the two stages of prayer I have already described. We can name them: reverent recital of the customary rule of prayer with feeling and attention, is followed by teaching the soul to ascend to God by reflecting on divine things in such a way that we turn everything to the glory of God. This leads us to appeal to God frequently from the heart.

* * *

We pray morning and evening. The time between is long. However ardently we pray, if we turn to God only at these times in the whole day and night, it will all become scattered again. Then, when the time for prayer comes round, the soul will again be as cold and empty as before. Even if we pray fervently, if we then keep cooling down and becoming distracted, what profit is there in it? We just create and destroy, create and destroy again: it is no more than empty labour.

But if we now put ourselves to the task of not only of accomplishing our rule of prayer with attention and feeling, morning and night, but more: of practicing reflection on divine things, of turning every action to the glory of God, of frequently appealing to God from our heart with short, prayerful exclamations - then these long intervals between morning and evening, and between evening and morning prayers, will be filled with frequent appeals to God, and with frequent prayerful actions.

* * *

Although this is not unceasing prayer, it will be repeated often in such a way that, the more often it is repeated, the closer it will grow to unceasing prayer. This work is an inevitable and necessary transitional stage on the way to achievement of unceasing prayer.

If you carry out this work every day, constantly and without tiring, you can see for yourself what must happen in your soul!

From meditation on the divine, the fear of God will be born. This fear of God is already an achievement. In it, we understand the everlasting perfection of the actions of God - comprehending them through both thought and feeling.

By turning our every action to the glory of God, we will bear within ourselves the constant remembrance of God. Remembering, whatever we do, that we are constantly in the presence of God, we will actually be walking in the presence of God.

Finally, by frequent appeals to God ... in other words, by often evoking reverent feelings toward God in our hearts, we will give birth to the constant warm and loving utterance in our heart of the sweet name of our Lord. In turn, this will inevitably kindle in our hearts the spiritual fire about which I spoke earlier. This (inner fire) brings with it a profound peace, constant watchfulness, and life-giving courage. With it we will enter into that state which is the highest we can aspire to on earth, a true foretaste of the state of bliss awaiting us all in the future.

This is a true realization of what the apostle described when he said: *"Your life is hid with Christ in God."* (Colossians 3:3).

* * *

When you begin to possess yourself in this way - possessing yourself in your heart as the body possesses itself when it is surrounded on all sides by warmth ...

Or when you begin to conduct yourself as people do in the presence of a great and important personage - with fear and attention, unwilling to offend in anything even when they have permission to walk and act freely ...

Then you will see begin in your soul the same reaction to the Lord that a bride may have toward a beloved bridegroom ...

And then you will know that the precious guest of our souls is very near the door; so that He will come to you and dwell within you.

I think that these few instructions are enough to guide those who search energetically. But really, all this is said only to let those of you who labour in prayer know what is the final end of your prayer. Otherwise, having laboured little and achieved little, you may think you have achieved all that is possible, and then you may relax and weaken in your efforts. This will halt your further ascent on the steps of prayer.

* * *

On the roads, there are signposts to let travellers know how far they have come, and how far they have still to go. In the same way, in our spiritual life, there are similar signs which mark out the steps to perfection. These are provided in order that, knowing where they started, those who are eager for perfection should know how far they have still to go. Then they will not halt half way, so denying themselves the fruits of their work, fruits which - if they would only take one or two more turnings - are perhaps waiting only just round the corner.

Now I will close my sermon with an ardent prayer, asking that the Lord may give you wisdom in everything, and that you may all reach the perfection of man according to the measure of your age in Christ.

AMEN

THE FOURTH SERMON

A life of prayer

I have now spoken to you about techniques of prayer three times:

1. About the method of reciting prayers with attention.
2. About the method of ascending to God with mind and heart in accord.
3. And about the method of standing constantly in the presence of God with burning spirit.

In order that everyone can take part in the blessing of prayer to the measure of his capacity, the Lord has showed us different steps and different kinds of prayer. Because the work of prayer is a great labour, it is, as I said earlier, the proof of the life of spirit, as well as its food. Because of this, above all else, we should strive for perfection in prayer.

* * *

I have described to you briefly how you can succeed in different kinds of prayer. Now I want to add to that a reminder, and also a warning, for it is difficult and even almost impossible to succeed in prayer if one does not at the same time strive for other virtues.

If we compare prayer to a perfume, and the soul to a flask, it becomes clear that just as it is impossible to store a perfume in a flask that is full of holes, so, in a soul which lacks many of the virtues and which is therefore not whole, it is impossible to preserve the perfume of prayer.

If we compare a man of prayer to the structure of the body, we can learn the following lesson: just as - for example - a man with only one leg cannot walk, even if the rest of his body is in good health, so a man who is not active in good works cannot come near to God, nor can he reach Him in prayer. Penetrate to the heart of the apostolic teachings, and you will see that they never speak of prayer alone. It is always accompanied by good works. For example, listen how the Apostle Paul summons the Christian to the spiritual struggle and arms him with all the weapons of God.

Examine what these weapons are. The Christian must:
- Gird his loins with Truth and put on the breastplate of Righteousness.
- His feet must be shod with the Truth of the gospel of Peace.
- His shield is Faith.
- His helmet is Hope.
- His sword is the Word of God. (Ephesians.6:14-17)

These are your weapons!

Only as a result of all this has he established his warrior in prayer, as in a fortress, about whom he says: *"praying always with all prayer and supplication in the Spirit."* (Ephesians 6: 18)

It is only by prayer - of course - that all the enemies can be overcome. But before we can be strong in prayer, we must succeed in Faith, in Hope, and in Knowledge of the Truth, in Truthfulness - and in everything else.

* * *

In another place the same apostle, investing the soul with wedding garments, as if it were the bride of Christ, says:

"Put on a heart of compassion, kindness, humility, meekness, longsuffering, forgiveness of one another, love, peace - and the Word of God in wisdom." (Colossians 3: 12-16).

Then, like a crowning virtue, he puts prayer at the head:

"... teaching and admonishing one another with psalms, with hymns and spiritual songs, singing - with grace in your hearts - unto God."

In many other places in the Word of God, prayer is placed in absolute interdependence with all good works, regarded as their queen to whom all of them minister, and who calls them all to follow her. Better still, she is known as their fragrant blossom. As the blossom - in order to catch the eye - must stand out from leaf and branch, trunk and root, so prayer, the blossom of the soul, surpasses its entourage of virtues and good works, as if they were its roots. Faith is its trunk, Charity forms the branches, and spiritual and physical labours are its leaves.

When such a tree is rooted in our soul, it will blossom with prayer all day long, filling the whole temple within us with its fragrance.

* * *

All this I am bringing back to your memory, so that none of you should think that simply because you labour in prayer, that is enough. It is not. We must be eager to care for all things and to perfect ourselves in every good work.

It is true that we cannot succeed in works without prayer. But works must be practiced in addition to prayer - and with the support of prayer. We must even pray for success in prayer. In practice, the work of prayer is as essential as is the work of good actions.

To achieve all this, we must take pains over everything, and demonstrate continual diligence. It is the same as with a clock. When the clock goes well, it shows the correct time. For this, every little wheel and every other inside part must be whole, correctly positioned, and properly interconnected. It is the same with the internal mechanisms of our soul: like the hand of a clock, the aim of our spirit can be pointed to the right or wrong place. It is right when it points straight to God, and this is when all the parts of the soul are whole and are correctly oriented, so to speak, each performing their proper task.

But exactly what kind of good works are needed to support a life of prayer? What sort of prayerfully active life should the Christian arrange for himself. I will tell you this not in my own words, but in the words of Saint Demitrius of Rostov, who gives the following very concise instructions. I beg you to attend to this:

1. *"Having risen from sleep,"* he says, *"let your first thought be of God, your first word and prayer directed to God, creator and sustainer of your life, who has forever the power to kill or bring to life, to strike or to heal, to save or to let perish.*

2. *"Prostrate yourself and give thanks to God, who has wakened you from sleep, and has not allowed you to perish in your lawlessness, but patiently awaits your return.*

3. *"Make a turn to the better, by saying with the psalmist: 'I remembered the works of the Lord'* (Psalm76:11)*, for the good Way to heaven cannot be properly trodden except by those who begin each day well.*

4. *"From early morning, be a Seraphim in prayer, a Cherubim in action, and an Angel in attitude.*

5. *"From this point in life onwards, waste no time, but attend only to what is necessary.*

6. *"In all your actions, all your words, all your deliberations, keep your mind in God: do not have anything in mind but Christ, so that no other image may touch your clean heart except the pure image of Christ, your God and Saviour.*

7. *"Arouse yourself to the love of God by every possible means, especially by repeating to yourself with the psalmist: 'My heart grew hot within me, and in my meditation a fire was kindled.'* (Psalm 38:4).

8. *"If you wish to love God unceasingly, look on his presence continually with your inner eye, and for His sake abandon every evil deed, word, and thought. For this reason you must do everything honestly, speak honestly, and think honestly, humbly, and in awe of the Son.*

9. *"Meekness should go together with praise, humility and honesty.*

10. *"A quiet and humble word should be truthful and useful, but when you are silent, think over the words you are going to say. An idle or harmful word should never pass your lips.*

11. *"If you laugh, laugh always with a smile, and not too often.*

12. *"Be watchful in yourself against rage, arrogance, and argumentativeness. If you are angry, control yourself.*

13. *"Be always moderate in food and drink.*

14. *"Be generous in all things, and God will bless you while people will praise you.*

15. *"Death is the end of all things, so it should be always in your prayers."*

You can see from this what a steady life is prescribed for the Christian man of prayer.

* * *

It is true that these rules speak mostly of prayer, of mindful and heartfelt approaches to God, but a number of other virtues are also mentioned. Without these particular virtues prayer cannot be sustained. This is something everyone will discover for himself in practice - if only he starts practicing prayer in the right way. How can you start to pray if you are burdened by lack of self control, if you are confused by anger or annoyance, if you are not at peace with someone, or if you are absentminded with worries and distractions.

If none of these exist in you, then their opposite virtues will be present. This is why Saint John Lestvichnik says - when speaking about prayer - that it is both the mother and the daughter of virtue.

* * *

Some of you, when you hear this, may think: *"That is so much to expect of us! What a difficult and heavy burden! Where can we find the time and the strength for all this?"*

Take courage, brothers! What is needed is not so very much. Just one thing is necessary: fervour towards God, with the desire that one's soul be saved by Him.

By nature, there is much good in the soul. The difficulty is that it becomes overlaid with so much that is bad. As soon as fervour to please God and for salvation is born in the soul, all its natural goodness will collect around this fervour, and much that is good will appear in the soul. Then this fervour - strengthened by God's blessing and reinforced by this dormant goodness - will begin to develop other good qualities and enrich itself. Step by step, it will grow.

This fervour contains the seed of true prayer in itself. At first, it is nourished by our natural goodness. Then it begins to be nourished by the goodness we have acquired. So it will grow in strength, and will start to praise God, and - as it increases in its growth – it will begin to sing to Him with a varied and blessedly prayerful song in the heart.

May the Lord help you to achieve this.

AMEN

FOUR SERMONS
ON PRAYER

PART TWO

SOME PRAYERS
OF THE FATHERS

SOME PRAYERS
OF THE FATHERS

This section of the book contains a brief selection of patristic prayers from many different sources, intended to help the reader who wishes to begin learning how to put these ideas into practice.

Saint Theophan's conception of the origin of these prayers, and a further glimpse of how he imagines they may be used and what this may lead to, is described in the passage below.

"When this thought or contemplation visits the inner temple of our spirit," wrote Theophan once, *"this is filled with the light and majesty of God. The spirit's rapture then is indescribable. All its bones, that is, all the smallest moving parts of its being, give an irrepressible leap of deep inward joy, exclaiming as it were: 'How glorious is our Lord and God!'.*

"This bliss of the spirit at its contemplation of the perfection of God becomes an inner doxology spontaneously offered up by the spirit to God as a 'sacrifice of praise'. Glorification of God in words is the fruit of this joy and in itself is of a lower order, not only incommensurable with God but even with what is felt in the spirit. 'But no single word will suffice for singing Thy wonders'. We must include every song that praises God. 'Praise of God in the spirit is a most comforting state of joy and spiritual gladness,'

"All of this is wakened only by the fact that God is such that he inspires praise. This praise can be awakened by every perfection of God, and by each of His deeds - even by those that relate to us personally - but in this act of true praise every other consideration is set aside: one sees only God himself and the perfection of His acts.

"This is an entirely selfless sacrifice. It can be said that it is the true life of our spirit; our true communion with the divine life. Just as in our fear we are penetrated by God and kindled, as it were, with the fire of divinity, so in praising God in this way our spirit is penetrated by or taken up in God and communes with His beatitude.

"To ascend to this state, or to seek or desire to be raised to it is as natural and fruitful for the spirit as it is obligatory. It is in this condition that our Lord and God is given His due. That is why in so many places God's word tells us to praise the Lord, and why so many examples are given of this praise. Each of the saints who ascended to this state portrayed God's perfections in words and left behind their songs of praise for us. To read these songs with true depth and intensity is a necessity. It is the beginning or part of the fulfillment of our duty to praise God. No other way than with these songs can a man ascend to the inward, spiritual praise of God. These are his educators. They should not be abandoned, even when the inner life has been cultivated.

"In order to reach up high one must have a ladder. One does not throw away a ladder after climbing it once, because one will need it again.

"Our praise should begin each time with the songs that have been given to us - and then fall silent when the spirit begins to sing praises. In practice the praises should dwell either on the all-perfect nature of God or on one or other of His perfections - or it should pass from one to another of these. This must not be a cold contemplation of the qualities of God: it must contain a living awareness of them." Then he gives a test of success in this 'true contemplation,' that it must come: *"with joy and rapture because this is the nature of God.*

"It is salutary if we can put ourselves in this state as often as possible. There is no better way than this of cleansing the spirit from all earthly admixtures and from everything sensory - because in this activity it will be allowed to taste a sweetness with which nothing else can be compared."

A PRAYER TO GOD FOR MERCY

by Saint Theophan

"We claim no right to mercy,
we do not deserve it.
We are sinners in everything,
in word and deed and thought
and in all our feelings.
But we are sorry and we pray to God
to be merciful to us sinners!'

If Your all-seeing eye sees
that our hearts are hard
and our resolution to do better is weak:
do You Yourself send us true contrition
and strengthen our sagging wills.
O God be merciful to us sinners!"

"We do not demand speedy deliverance,
we dare not say it will be a day,
a week, even a year;
but yielding wholly to thy will,
we make one prayer
'God be merciful to us sinners.'

"We dare not murmur before You,
but are now in such pain
that we shrink from a touch,
and as we cry like children in this pain,
we call: 'God be merciful to us sinners!'

"We are weak. Lord, do not allow us to fall
under the weight of misfortunes.
Give strength to our hearts
imbue us with hope,
so that despair may not defeat our spirit
- and God be merciful to us sinners!"

AMEN.

(From *The Heart of Salvation* - life and teachings of
Saint Theophan the Recluse - Praxis, 1992.)

AN INVOCATION TO
THE HOLY SPIRIT

by St. Symeon the New Theologian

Come, true light.
Come, life eternal.
Come, hidden mystery.
Come, treasure without name.
Come, reality beyond all words.
Come, person beyond all understanding.
Come, rejoicing without end.
Come, light that knows no evening.
Come, unfailing expectation of the saved.
Come, the raising of the fallen.
Come, the resurrection of the dead.
Come, O all-powerful,
for unceasingly You create,
refashion and change
all things by Your will alone.

Come, invisible,
whom none may touch and handle.
Come, You who remain unmoved,
yet every instant are in every movement;
You who draw close to us who live in hell,
yet remain higher than the heavens.
Come, Your Name fills our hearts with longing
and is ever on our lips;
yet who You are and what Your nature us,
we may neither say nor know.

Come, eternal joy.
Come unfading garland.
Come, purple vesture of our God and King.
Come belt of crystal
set with precious stones.
Come sandal that none dares to touch.
Come royal robe
and right hand of true sovereignty.
Come, for my wretched soul has ever longed
and ever longs for You.
Come, Alone to the alone,
for as You see I am alone:
You have separated me from all things
and made me to be alone upon the earth.
Come, for You Yourself are the desire
that is within me,
it is You who have made me long after You,
the wholly inaccessible.

Come, my breath and my life.
Come, the consolation of my humble soul.
Come, my joy, my glory, my endless delight.
I give thanks,
for You have become one spirit with me,
in a union without confusion.
Unchanging and unaltered,
God over all,
You have yet become all in all to me:
food inexplicable, freely bestowed,
ever nourishing my soul;
a fountain springing up within my heart,
a garment of light consuming the demons,
purification that washes me clean
through the immortal and holy tears
granted at Your coming to all whom You visit.

I give You thanks,
to me You are a light that knows
no evening, a sun that never sets.
You cannot remain hidden,
for You fill all things with your glory.
You never hide yourself from anyone,
but we always hide from You,
not wishing to come near You.
For where could You hide Yourself,
since You have no place
in which to take Your rest?
Or why should You hide,
since You turn away from no one
and are afraid of none?

Pitch Your tent within me,
gracious Master;
take up Your dwelling in me now
and remain in Your servant unceasingly,
inseparably, to the end.
At my departure from this life
and afterwards, may I be found in You
and reign with You, who are God over all.

Stay with me, Master,
do not leave me alone.
When they find You dwelling within me,
my enemies who seek always to devour my
soul, will be put to flight;
they will have no more power against me,
when they see You,
Who are more powerful than all
who lodge in the house of my humble soul.

You did not forget me, Master,
when I was in the world
and sunk in ignorance,
but You chose me
and separated me from the world
and set me in the presence of Your glory.
Keep me constant and unshaken
in the interior dwelling-place
that You have made within me.

Though dead,
I live when I gaze on You;
possessing You, though poor,
I am forever rich,
more wealthy than any ruler.
Eating and drinking You,
clothing myself in You from day to day,
I shall be filled with blessings and delight beyond all telling.
For You are every blessing
and all splendour and joy,
and to You is due glory,
to the Holy, Consubstantial and Life-giving Trinity,
worshipped and confessed by all the faithful
and adored in Father, Son and Holy Spirit,
now and ever, and to the ages of ages.

AMEN.

(Translated by Bishop Kallistos of Diokleia: (Kallistos Ware). Reproduced from *Eastern Churches Review. Vol. V. No. 2. Autumn 1973.)*

A PRAYER FROM NICODEMUS
OF THE HOLY MOUNTAIN

O Lord my God!
I sing and praise Your ineffable glory
and Your infinite greatness.
I thank You that by Your goodness alone
You have given me to exist
and to share in the life-saving blessings
of Your dispensation by incarnation,
that You have often saved me from calamities
that threatened me even without my knowledge,
and have delivered me from the hands
of my unseen foes.

I confess to You that countless times
I have stifled my conscience,
I have fearlessly transgressed Your holy
commandments
showing myself ungrateful for Your manifold
bounties.

O my most merciful Lord,
let my ingratitude not be too great
for Your mercy,
but overlook my sins and trespasses,
look with kindness on my tears of contrition,
and by the multitude of Your tender mercies
help me even now.

Grant me what is needful for my salvation,
and guide my life towards pleasing You
so that, unworthy as I am,
I too may glorify Your holy name.

AMEN.

A PRAYER OF
SAINT EPHRAIM

O Lord and Master of my life,
grant me not a spirit of sloth, despondency,
lust for power, and idle talk;

But grant to me Thy servant a spirit of sobriety,
humility, patience and love;

Yea, O Lord my King,
grant me to see my own transgressions,
instead of judging my brother,
for blessed art Thou unto the ages of ages.

AMEN.

PRAYERS OF
ST. JOHN THE ELDER

I

You who are hidden and concealed within me,
reveal within me
Your hidden mystery; manifest to me
Your beauty that is within me.
O You who have built me
as a temple for You to dwell in,
cause the cloud of Your glory
to overshadow inside Your temple,
so that the ministers of Your sanctuary
may cry out, in love for You, 'holy,'
as an utterance which burns in fire and spirit,
in a sharp stirring which is commingled with wonder
and astonishment,
activated as a living movement
by the power of Your being.

AMEN

II.

O Christ, the ocean of our forgiveness,
allow me to wash off in You
the dirt I am clothed in,
so that I may become resplendent
in the raiment of Your holy light.
May I be covered with the cloud
of Your hidden glory,
full of secret mysteries.
May the things which divert me
from gazing upon Your beauty
not be visible to me.
May wonder at Your glory
captivate me continually,
may my mind become unable to set in motion
worldly impulses.
May nothing ever separate me from Your love,
but rather may that desire,
which is in You,
to behold Your countenance
harrow me continually.

AMEN.

A MORNING PRAYER
TO THE HOLY TRINITY

By Saint John Chrysostom

Glory to You, our God, glory to You.
Glory to You, O Lord, our God,
Who always overlooks our sins.
Glory to You,
O Lord our God,
who enabled me to see this day.
Glory to You,
O most-holy Trinity, our God.
I venerate Your ineffable goodness.
I praise Your inexplorable forbearance.
I thank and glorify Your infinite mercy.
For although I deserve
every punishment and chastisement,
You have mercy and do good to me
With myriads of blessings.
Glory to You,
O Lord, my God,
for everything.

AMEN

(Adapted from *Voices in the Wilderness, An Anthology of Patristic Prayers*, Holy Cross Orthodox Press.)

SOME SHORT PRAYERS

from St. Isaac the Syrian

I

O Christ, fulfillment of the truth,
let Your truth rise in our hearts.
Let us know how to walk Your way
according to Your will.

II

O Lord fill my heart with life eternal.

III

O Lord, make me worthy to hate my life,
for the sake of life in You.

IV

O Lord, my God, You will illumine my darkness.

V

According to Thy will, O Lord, let it
be done to me.

AMEN.

(Adapted from *Voices in the Wilderness, An Anthology of Patristic Prayers,* Holy Cross Orthodox Press.)

A PRAYER OF THE SIXTH HOUR

by St. Sarrah

O Lord
You who measured
the heights and the earth
in the hollow of Your hand,
and created the six-winged Seraphim
to cry out to You with unceasing voice:
Holy, Holy, Holy,
glory to Your name,
Deliver me
from the mouth of the evil one, O Master.
Forget my many evil deeds
and through the multitude of Your compassions
grant me daily forgiveness
for You are blessed to all the ages.

AMEN.

FROM ST. MARDARIOS

O Master and God,
Father almighty,
Lord, and only-begotten Son,
Jesus Christ, and Holy Spirit,
one divinity and power,
have mercy on me a sinner,
and save me, Your unworthy servant,
in any way You know;
for You are blessed unto the ages of ages.

AMEN.

(From *The Syriac Fathers on Prayer and the Spiritual Life* by
Sebastian Brock. Cistercian Publications, Kalamazoo, Michigan.)

PRAYER BEFORE
COMMUNION

By Saint Symeon the new Theolgian

Wash me with my tears, O Word,
and with them cleanse me,
pardon my offences
and grant me forgiveness.

You know how many are my transgressions
But you also know my wounds,
see my bruises, recognize my faith,
observe my eagerness, and hear my sighs.
Nothing escapes you, O my God -
my creator, my redeemer -
no single tear, nor part of one.

Your eyes have known my original nature.
The deeds I have yet to commit
are already written in your book.
Look upon my lowliness,
see how much I work
And forgive, O God of all, all my sins
so that with a pure heart,
a trembling mind, a contrite soul
I may take part in your immaculate
and all pure mysteries
in which all who eat and drink you
with a sincere heart
are deified and given life.

You have said, O my Master;
"Whoever eats my flesh
and drinks my blood
abides in Me, and I in him."

True indeed is this word
of my Master and my God,
for those who take in
the divine and deifying graces
are no longer alone;
they are with you, O Christ,
the light of the triple sun
that illumines the world.

So that I may not remain alone
or be parted from you,
the giver of life, my breath,
my life, my delight,
and salvation of the world.

Therefore I have drawn near you
with tears and contrite soul.
I entreat you to receive me
as a ransom for my errors,
that without condemnation
I may partake of your life-giving
and immaculate mysteries:
that as you have said
you may remain with me,
the thrice-wretched one;

AMEN.

PRAYERS BEFORE COMMUNION

By Saint John Chrysostom

I

I believe, O Lord, and I confess
That thou art truly the Christ,the Son
of the living God, who came into the world
to save sinners, of whom I am first.
And I believe that this is indeed Thy pure Body,
and Thy precious Blood.
Therefore, I pray to you: Have mercy on me
And forgive me my transgressions,
voluntary and involuntary,in word and in deed,
in knowledge or in ignorance;
and make me worthy to partake without condemnation
of Thy Holy Mysteries,
for remission of sins and life eternal.

AMEN.

II

Of Thy Mystical Supper, O Son of God
Today admit me as a communicant;
For I will not tell Thy Mystery to Thine
enemies,
nor give thee a kiss like Judas,
but like the thief I will confess thee:
Remember me, Lord,
When Thou comest into Thy kingdom.

Not unto judgment nor unto condemnation
be the partaking of thy Holy Mysteries to me, O
Lord,
but unto the healing of soul and body.

AMEN.

PRAYERS BEFORE COMMUNION

From St. Simeon Metaphrastes

I

You have smitten me with yearning, O Christ,
and with Your divine love You have changed me;
burn away my sins with Your spiritual fire
and make me worthy to be filled with Your joy;
that, rejoicing in Your goodness
I may magnify Your two comings.
How shall I the unworthy
Enter the glorious company of Your saints?
If I too dare to go into the festive chamber,
my robe betrays me, since it is not a festive garment,
and I shall be bound by the Angels and cast out.
So cleanse my soul from pollution, O Lord,
and of Your compassion save me.

AMEN.

II

Behold, I walk towards Holy Communion;
O Creator,
You are the fire which burns the unworthy.
Cleanse me from every stain.
And do not burn me
If I take part in it.

AMEN.

(Adapted from *a Manual of Eastern Orthodox Prayers.* Fellowship
of St.Alban & St.Sergius.)

PRAYERS BEFORE COMMUNION

By Saint Ioannikos the Great

O Father, my hope;
O Son my refuge;
O Holy Spirit, my protection:
O Holy Trinity, glory be to Thee.

The Father is my hope,
the Son is my refuge,
the Holy Spirit is my shelter;
O Holy Trinity, glory to You.

To you, O Mother of God
I commit all my hope
keep me under your protection.

AMEN

(Adapted from *a Manual of Eastern Orthodox Prayers*. Fellowship
of St.Alban & St.Sergius.)

THE PRAYER OF
JOSEPH THE VISIONARY

TO YOU BE PRAISE
First-born of Being,
exalted and full of awe,
for, by the sacrifice of Your body,
You have effected salvation for the world.

O Christ, Son from the Holy Father,
to You do I pray in awe at this time;
of You, Lord do I ask Your will
and beseech Your compassion,
that my whole person may be made holy
through Your grace,
and that the enemy's constraint upon me
may be rendered ineffective.

Purify my understanding
in Your compassion,
so that my hands may stretch out in purity
to receive Your holy and fearful Body and Blood.

Cleanse my hidden mind
with the hyssop of Your grace,
for I draw near to the Holy of Holies of Your Mysteries.

Wash from me all understanding
that belongs to the flesh,
and may an understanding which belongs to Your Spirit
be mingled within my soul.

Cause to reside in me
a faith that beholds Your Mysteries,
so that I may behold Your sacrifice
as You are, and not as I am.

Create eyes in me, and so may I see with Your eyes,
for I cannot see with my own eyes.
May my mind travel inwards
towards the hiddenness of Your sacrifice,
just as You have travelled out into the open
and been conjoined to Your Mysteries.

At this moment
may I be totally forgetful of myself,
and remain utterly unmindful
of my own person.

May every bodily image
be wiped away from my mind's eye,
and may You alone
be depicted before the eye of my mind.
And now, when your Spirit descends from heaven
upon Your Mysteries,
may I ascend in spirit from earth to heaven.

At this time
when Your power is mingled in with the bread,
may my life be commingled
with Your spiritual life.

At this moment
when the wine is changed and becomes Your blood,
may my thoughts be inebriated
with the commixture of Your love.

At this time
when Your Lamb is lying slain upon the altar,
may sin cease
and be utterly removed from all my limbs.

At this moment
when Your Body is being offered
as a sacrifice to Your Father,
may I too be a holy sacrifice
to You and to Him who sent You,
and may my prayer ascend before You
together with the prayer of Your priest.

Provide me with hidden hands
so that with them I may carry the fiery Coal.

Create in me a pure heart
so that Your holy power may reside within me,
so that, through the power of Your Spirit
I may in a spiritual fashion
inhale Your salvation.

Fashion in me, Lord,
eyes within my eyes
so that with new eyes
I may contemplate Your divine sacrifice.

Lord, may I not see
the outward aspect of what I am now to receive,
but hold me worthy to see and recognize,
as did Simon the fisherman
who was called blessed for his faith.

Lord, may I taste not just the bread in Your Body,
or just the cup in Your Blood:
give me faith so that I may see Your Body
and not the bread,
and drink Your living Blood from the cup.

Grant me that spiritual palate
which is able to taste Your Blood
and not the wine.
Wipe out from me
all the signs of my bodily nature,
and mark in me
the signs of Your spiritual nature.

May I draw near to You,
and You alone be seen by me:
may I not perceive anything else that is next to me,
but may I walk in the house of prayer
as though in heaven,
and may I receive You
who live in the highest heaven.

You made me into a spiritual being
when You gave me rebirth from the baptismal water;
make me a spiritual being now too,
as I draw near to receive You.

It is a matter of great awe, Lord,
that Your Body and Your Blood,
O Christ our Saviour,
should be consumed and drunk
with that same mouth which receives
ordinary natural food and drink.

Lord, You did not give to the spiritual beings
what I am receiving now:
stir up within me at this time, Lord,
the sense of wonder at Your Cross;
fill me with a fervour of faith at this moment,
so that my thoughts may be inflamed
with the fire of Your love;
and may my eyes become for You
rivulets of water
to wash all my limbs;
may Your hidden love
be infused into my thoughts,
so that my hidden thoughts
may flow for You
with tears and groans.

May my body be sanctified by You,
may my soul shine out for You.

May my body be purified by You
of every image and form here on earth,
and may my thoughts be cleansed by You,
and my limbs be sanctified by You;
and my understanding shine out,
and may my mind be illumined by You.
May my person become a holy temple for You;
may I be aware in my whole being of Your majesty.
May I become a womb for You in secret:
then do You come and dwell in me by night
and I will receive You openly,
taking delight spiritually
in the Holy of Holies of my thoughts.
Then shall I take delight in Your Body and Your
Blood in my limbs.

You have revealed to me Your hiddenness
in the Bread and in the Wine,
reveal in me Your love,
cause a desire for You to shine out in me,
so that I may receive Your Body in love for You
and in desire for You I may drink your Blood.

With the fulfilment of the sacrifice of Yourself,
fulfill my request and accept my prayer;
harken to my words and sign all my limbs,
hidden and revealed.

Lord, I shall openly sign all my limbs
with the sign of Your Cross,
as You have said, do You, Lord,
mark me in a hidden way
with the truth of your Cross.

May I receive You
not into the stomach which belongs to the body's limbs,
but into the womb of my mind,
so that You may be conceived there,
as in the womb of the virgin.

And may You be revealed in me
through the spiritual works
and good deeds that are pleasing to Your will.

Through consuming You,
may all my lusts be brought to an end;
through drinking Your cup
may all my passions be quenched.
May my thoughts take strength
from Your sustenance,
and through the living Blood of Your revered passion
may I receive strength for the course
of the service of righteousness.

May I grow in a hidden way
and openly prevail.
May I run eagerly
and attain the measure of the Hidden Person,
May I become someone perfected,
made complete in all my spiritual limbs,
my head crowned with the crown of the perfection
of all the spiritual limbs.
May I become a royal diadem in Your hands,
as You promised O true Lord,
Sovereign of all stirrings, Lord of all powers,
God almighty.

May I be intermingled with You
and with Your love and Your longing
on that day when Your majesty will shine out,
and when the words find fulfilment that say
'To You shall every knee bow.
and it is You that every tongue
in heaven and on earth and beneath the earth shall
confess.'

And along with the spiritual beings
and all who have loved Your revelation in spirit,
may I confess You, praise You, exalt You
in that kingdom which does not ever dissolve
or pass away.
Now and always.

AMEN

(From *The Syriac Fathers on Prayer and the Spiritual Life* by Sebastian
Brock. Cistercian Publications, Kalamazoo, Michigan.)

A PRAYER TO THE
HOLY SPIRIT

O Heavenly King, Comforter,
the Spirit of truth,
Who art everywhere present
and fillest all things;
treasury of blessings and giver of life,
come and abide in us.
Cleanse us from all impurity,
and of Thy goodness save our souls.

AMEN.

SAINT THEOPHAN
THE RECLUSE

His life in brief

As part of the celebrations of the Millennium of the Russian Church in 1988, Theophan the Recluse was canonized, so that he became Saint Theophan less than a hundred years after his death. Yet even today, few people in the English speaking world have heard of him, fewer know anything about his remarkable life, and practically nobody knows about his equally remarkable spiritual teachings - teachings which make him a true modern representative of the ancient tradition of the fathers of the church who mainly flourished between one thousand and two thousand years ago - a recent teacher of the ancient Christian knowledge of man that was at one time handed down by those early fathers.

Saint Theophan was a *'starets'*: an elder which in the Eastern Church means an experienced, inspired and enlightened teacher. He was one of the last - if not the last - of the bishops to teach the Church's ancient knowledge of man in public. For this reason his importance lies in his writings, some of the most recent and therefore most understandable texts from that ancient tradition - whose own importance is due to the fact that the Eastern Orthodox Church persists in following teachings unchanged since the first and second centuries of the Christian era - a closeness to the source that is important for those who wish to recover the vitality of early Christian spirituality.

Theophan the Recluse was born George Govorov, the son of a priest, and in his youth he lived steeped in an atmosphere of Orthodox Christianity. Early in his life he visited Kiev Lavra and was deeply impressed by the qualities manifested in the Kiev caves. In his youth he passed through the rigorous discipline of the Orel seminary, then went to Kiev Theological Academy where, in 1841 at the age of 26, he became both a Hieromonk and Master of Theology. His early career was not monastic, instead he worked as a schoolteacher within the Church - after which he made two major journeys abroad, one of which, to Jerusalem, lasted seven years and gave him ample opportunity to learn from the ancient Christian religious communities in and around the Holy Land - a fact that helps to explain the great erudition he demonstrated in later life - an erudition confirmed by the fact that after his death the majority of the works of the great fathers of the Church were found in his cell, as well as many philosophical books including Hegel, Jacobi and Schelling, together with a one hundred and fifty volume theological dictionary in French.

In 1857, when he returned from the second of these journeys, he briefly became Rector of St Petersburg Theological Academy. Then, in 1859. he became Bishop of Tambov. In his relatively short career as a bishop there, he made a powerful impression on his congregation. In 1863. Theophan became bishop of a larger diocese in the city of Vladimir, where he preached some notable sermons. In 1866 he resigned the Vladimir diocese and entered the monastery of Vysha as an anchorite. For the first six years in the monastery, he continued to some degree to participate in the life of the community, but in 1872, after six years in the monastery, he finally withdrew into his cell and was no longer accessible to visitors.

Even after this, Theophan the Recluse used to receive twenty to forty letters every day - and he answered every one himself, so that until his death he continued to help and guide people by correspondence. In this way he left us a real wealth of religious and philosophical teachings, not only theoretical but often thoroughly practical. Also in this time he wrote a number of important books, including two commentaries on the scriptures - and also edited two of the most important books on spirituality possessed by the Russian Church. From 1876 to 1890 Theophan led the translation and adaptation from Church Slavonic into Russian of the *Dobrotolubiye*, the Russian version of the *Philokalia*, the great Greek text of the writings of the early fathers, to which he added certain texts from the Syrian fathers. The result, printed in five quarto volumes, remains one of the great spiritual classics of the world. During this time, Theophan adapted and considerably changed the book now known as *'Unseen Warfare'*, originally written by a Venetian priest, Lorenzo Scupoli, in the sixteenth century, and previously edited into Greek by Nicodemus of the Holy Mountain. Some chapters in the modern version are entirely the work of Theophan. [2]

In 1891, Theophan the Recluse died in his cell at the age of 76, Thus passed the man who said: *"Do not gravitate to the earth. All is corruptible; only the happiness beyond the grave is eternal, unchanging and true, and this happiness depends upon how we spend this life of ours!"* When all who wished had bowed to the remains of Theophan, the coffin was taken to Kazan Cathedral and there it was buried in a vault on the right-hand side in the Vladimir Chapel. A vast crowd of people who had been unable to get into the Church for the funeral service attended the burial, weeping and mourning. As the funeral procession passed, many groups of men joined it, carrying the traditional birch-bark bags of the pilgrim over their shoulders. Some had walked 200 versts, some 300, in order to pay their respects to him, to pray that his soul should be released, and to ask his prayers for them before the throne of God.

In 1988 Theophan the Recluse was canonized as part of the celebrations for the millennium of the Russian Orthodox Church. Yet even today the life of Theophan the Recluse remains in many ways a closed book. The one person who could have told us most about the details of Theophan's life, the person closest to him, outlived him by only a short while. This was his kelinik (cell attendant) Evlampy, who had served him for twenty-five years. Evlampy fasted for ten days after Theophan's death, and he himself died within two weeks of the bishop. Because of this, little is known about the last days of Theophan's life.

Sergius Bolshakoff, the Russian author of the book *"Russian Mystics,"*[1] devoted the tenth chapter of this book to Theophan the Recluse, whom he calls the greatest Russian writer on mystical subjects, not only in the Nineteenth Century, but throughout Russian history.

---

1)- *Unseen Warfare* - edited by Nicodemus of the Holy Mountain and revised by Theophan the Recluse. Mowbrays, London.)

2)- Cf. *Russian Mystics* - by Sergius Bolshakoff, Cistercian Studies, 26, Cistercian Publications, Kalamazoo, Michigan, Passim.

PRAXIS

BOOKS ON ESOTERIC CHRISTIANITY, CHRISTIAN MYSTICISM, AND RELATED SUBJECTS

Saint Theophan the Recluse

THE HEART OF SALVATION

The life and teachings of Theophan the Recluse, greatest of Russia's masters of inner Christianity, compiler of the fullest version of the Russian 'Philokalia'. The book draws on seven years of study in the ancient monasteries of the Middle East and is rooted in the richly practical spirituality of 19th Century Russia. It is of great practical significance to serious students of hesychastic spirituality.

ISBN 1-872292-02-X

208PP PB$19.95 £14.95

THE PATH OF PRAYER

St.Theophan's Four Sermons on Prayer

A full and rich introduction to the use of daily and liturgical prayer as a method of spiritual development by this researcher, bishop, hermit and staretz whose correspondence guided thousands.

ISBN 1-872292-14-3 96 PP PB $11.95, £9.95

HARDBOUND $15.95, £11.95

TURNING WITHIN

BY THOMAS JOHNSON-MEDLAND

In this little book by an American Orthodox Deacon you will find a familiar voice speaking of 'interior prayer.' What the author has learned can help others to pray.

ISBN 1-872292-21-6, 45 PP, PB, $9.95 £7.50

PRAXIS MONOGRAPHS

BY BORIS MOURAVIEFF

NO.1 THE PROBLEM OF THE NEW MAN

A clear vision of the dangers of our current course, and an outline of possibilities for an individual regeneration that could assist in avoiding such a catastrophe.

ISBN 1-872292-20-8 $5.95 £3.95

NO 2. THE SUBSTANTIAL AND THE ESSENTIAL

A further study of the problem of individual regeneration defining the task of the seeker at this crucial point in history.

ISBN 1-872292-21-6 $5.95 £3.95

NO.3   OUSPENSKY , GURDJIEFF AND FRAGMENTS

Examines the relation between G.I.Gurdjieff and P.D.Ouspensky, drawing on Boris Mouravieff's close friendship with Ouspensky.

ISBN 1-872292-22-4 $9.95 £5.95

NO.4 BELIEFS OF THE PRE-CHRISTIAN SLAVS

Describes the remarkable similarities between the doctrines of the pre-Christian religion of the Slavic peoples, and the classical inner forms of early Christian tradition

ISBN B-872292-22-4 $5.95 £3.95

NO.5 LIBERTY, EQUALITY, FRATERNITY

The famous slogan of the French Revolution and its narrowing effect on world thought, suggesting that a change in the order of words might might actually have given our modern world a different sense of priorities.

ISBN B-872292-23-2 $5.95 £3.95

....

A METHOD OF PRAYER FOR MODERN TIMES
by Eugraph Kovalevsky

A lucid manual for methods of prayer used by the Russian Church - in a form once given by the author to prayer groups in the French Orthodox church and hence admirably suited to contemporary Western seekers.

ISBN 1-872292-18-6   PB $19.95 £13.95

*A new translation reveals the spiritual science
of the early fathers.*

THE TRIADS OF
ST. GREGORY PALAMAS

Introduction by the Translator, Praxis Director Robin Amis

This unique book, Saint Gregory Palamas' Triads, is of great philosophical, spiritual and historical importance. It deals with the difference between spiritual and scientific knowledge; the Christian enlightenment; prayer of the heart, and the method of circular attention; describing the Transfiguration as a type of true charismatic experience and early ideas of how the Age to Come can be reached in this life.

ISBN 1-872292-15-1 160PP PB $19.95   £14.95

by P.D.Ouspensky
THE COSMOLOGY OF MAN'S
POSSIBLE EVOLUTION

Published with the help of his senior pupils, the only publication of the second series of O's lectures, introducing the important cosmological aspect of his personal teaching.

COSMOLOGICAL LECTURES   PB   ISBN 1-872292-01-1 £14.95
WITH PSYCHOLOGICAL LECTURES HC ISBN 1-872292-00-3 £24.95

by Boris Mouravieff
GNOSIS - STUDY AND COMMENTARIES ON
THE ESOTERIC TRADITION OF EASTERN ORTHODOXY

An ancient Christian spiritual tradition illuminates the inner spiritual doctrines of the early church. These three volumes address the meaning of human life and history, and its relation to divine purpose and cosmic processes. Boris Mouravieff's Gnosis provides practical information on the development of the heart and the transformation of spiritual energies.

VOL.I EXOTERIC CYCLE ISBN 1-872292-10-0 296 P PB
· VOL.II MESOTERIC CYCLE, ISBN 1-872292-11-9 304 P PB
VOL.III ESOTERIC CYCLE, ISBN 1-872292-12-7 304 P PB   EACH
$37.50 £24.95 $89.95 £69.95 THE SET

TAPES FROM THE PHILOKALIA

Chosen by translator G.E.H. Palmer for a blind friend, read by Sergei Kadloubovsky from the original English translation of the 'Philokalia' published by Faber, these texts 'on watchfulness and holiness' are a meaningful and moving expression of the inner traditions of the early church fathers.

TWO 90 MIN. AUDIO TAPES : $19.95. £14.95

1000 YEARS ARE AS ONE DAY

A sensitive one-hour video documentary on the monasteries of Mount Athos, giving an in-depth view of life and liturgy in this remarkable spiritual community - made for German television, and now available in the US.

DISTRIBUTED BY PRAXIS ONLY IN USA - $50.00

by Robin Amis
A DIFFERENT CHRISTIANITY

After editing Mouravieff, Ouspensky and Theophan, Robin Amis, director of Praxis Institute, has finally written his own book, *A Different Christianity*, the distillation of more than fourteen years of research into traditional sources of the Royal Way, a Christian spiritual discipline little known to the Western world.

PAPER ISBN 0-791425-72-X $29.95   £24.50
HARDCOVER ISBN 0-791425-71-1 $59.90   £49.95

WHO WRITES THE WAVES?
40 years of poems by Robin Amis.

Often read in English poetry readings in the late sixties, these poems have an almost classical lyricism, and touch on the deepest questions of the inner life.

96 PAGES, HANDBND ISBN 1-872292-03-8 $19.95. £15.95

PRAXIS INSTITUTE PRESS

A DIVISION OF PRAXIS RESEARCH INSTITUTE, INC. A NON-PROFIT CORPORATION REGISTERED IN THE STATE OF MASSACHUSETTS

Web-page at www.praxisresearch.org - mail to

Three Barns, Aish Lane, South Brent, Devon. UK TQ10 9JF -

or: 2931 W. Belmont Ave. Chicago, IL 60618 USA

24hr US voicemail (847) 459-1990

e-Mail sales enquiries www.praxis.press@praxisresearch.org

Institute Information www.praxis.institute@praxisresearch.org